Jesus Goes Away

What the Bible Tells Us Series

The text of these books has been rewritten
on the basis of Today's English Version,
keeping as much of the New Testament stories
as can be understood by the intended readers.

Illustrations by Kees de Kort

First United States Paperback Edition 1980

Original Dutch Version © 1968
Netherlands Bible Society, Hilversum

English Text © 1978
British and Foreign Bible Society

International Standard Book No. 0-8066-1774-8

Manufactured in the United States of America

P250

AUGSBURG Publishing House
Minneapolis, Minnesota

After Jesus died
his friends saw him many times.
They saw that he was alive.

Jesus said to them,
"Do not go away from Jerusalem.
In a few days the Holy Spirit
will come to you.
When the Holy Spirit comes
you will be filled with power.
You will tell people about me.

You will tell people about me in Jerusalem.
You will tell people about me in Judaea.

You will tell people about me in Samaria.
You will tell people about me everywhere."

After Jesus said this he disappeared
into a cloud.

Jesus' friends were looking up into the sky.

Two men came to them.
The men wore white clothes.

The men said,
"Why are you looking for Jesus in the sky?
He is in heaven,
but he will come back."

Jesus' friends went back to the city.

They went to the room where they were staying.

They met together very often.

They met to pray to God.

It was soon Pentecost.
Pentecost was a special holiday.

People who lived in other countries
came to the city.

Jesus' friends were sitting in their room.
Suddenly there was a noise.
The noise was like the wind.

There was something like flames too.
The flames seemed to touch each person in the room.

The Holy Spirit had come.
The Holy Spirit made them able
to talk in other languages.
Jesus' friends spoke to people
from other countries.

They told the people
about all the things God had done.
The people were very surprised.

They were surprised to hear
Jesus' friends talking
in their languages.

Peter said,
"God's promise is for you.
God's promise is for your children.

God's promise is for all the people
whom God calls."